50 DEVOTIONALS
BORN IN FIRE
FORGED IN GOD'S LOVE
Book One

50 DEVOTIONALS
BORN IN FIRE
FORGED IN GOD'S LOVE
Book One

RED
DOOR
SENTINEL

DAVID A. JAGEMANN

Cover and graphics by Azure Summers Graphic Design
https://azuresgd.com

Author picture by Bruce Speidel
http://BruceSpeidel.com

DEDICATION

For my Mom and Dad who taught me the difference between right and wrong while lovingly giving me the freedom to figure it all out.

TABLE OF CONTENTS

Acknowledgments

First and foremost, I am thankful to my God who poured life through me in all possible circumstances and provided the ability to put the pieces together.

To my wife Tressa who has read much of my ramblings and still constantly supported me when I didn't want to continue – I can't thank you enough.

Thank you to my daughter Eliza who has been my shadow, pal, and source of joy.

Many thanks to my publisher Kelly Whitaker who has put up with me not knowing anything and always has the best advice to do everything.

Thank you to Destiny Writers for editing this project.

INTRODUCTION

Jesus said to them again, "Peace to you! As the Father has sent Me, I also send you."

John 20:21

My life, as described in these pages, is lived in the context of the Bible and directed by the hands of the One who loves me. The full expression of the struggles of life—illness, separation, death, and hardship—are found on each page, and will provide ample opportunity for believers to rejoice in God's glory as seen in their own lives.

These are unpretentious writings, coming from a life that has seen much. I am a work in progress, a humble servant, and one who finds himself living an answered prayer. That prayer was one that I prayed at the Sea of Galilee for a God-sized assignment and it has been a joy to live out the answer God gave me. I hope to encourage you, to make you laugh, and to remind you of the impact that each day can make in the one precious life you have been given to live.

I began writing twelve years ago and continue to this day. I still send letters out through the mail, as well as post on my Facebook page. These devotions are real, in-depth reflections of a life led by God, and no one else. I choose to lay down my life daily for my King but admittedly, I often want to quit. When you do what you were created to do, life becomes a great adventure; although, it is never easy.

The Bible is my only source for direction. It is not only a book to be reading, but also a book to be living, and a book for reflecting. I have found when life is perceived through the lens of the Word, much more is seen than remains hidden from sight.

Writing in his classic work *God in the Dock*, C.S. Lewis observed, "If you think of this world as a place intended simply for our happiness, you find it quite intolerable: think of it as a place of training and correction and it's not so bad."[1]

> Finally, believers, whatever is true, whatever is honorable *and* worthy of respect, whatever is right *and* confirmed by God's word, whatever is pure *and* wholesome, whatever is lovely *and* brings peace, whatever is admirable *and* of good repute; if there is any excellence, if there is anything worthy of praise, think *continually* on these things [**center your mind on them, and implant them in your heart**]. (Philippians 4:8, AMP, italics and bold added)

Enjoy what God has unselfishly given to me to give to you.

Steadfast (1 Cor 15:58),
Pastor Dave

I

FORGED

The refining pot is for silver & the furnace for gold, but the LORD tests the hearts.

Proverbs 17:3

"Born in fire, forged in God's love" is simple to say, but yet it is a complex and painful process. The beneficial fruit it produces cannot be denied. Rarely is ease the formula for our needs, whereas want is a diversion into the path of least resistance. The fire and the forge in God's hand, while directed by His love, culminates into a powerful product in our souls.

If we attempt to adjust the flame (heat) of the process (forge) or the amount of the breath it requires, then the result will be less than adequate; we become a product of our own fancy and our best falls to the worst. Substituting the heat with what we deem appropriate will pollute what is needed, leaving us with nothing but ease and pesky wants.

The fire and forge cannot be avoided in this world. Yet, the forge of God's love is the instrument that provides breath born of love—so that the lessons last. The striking is not left in the hands of an enemy or an individual who hammers out punishment for merely suffering and pain. Instead it attacks only in areas that need reshaping and that extreme measures can correct.

The result is a life that is honorable to behold and reflects the depth of God alone. The heat, melting, and twisting of souls are part of the process of living. We cannot deny the painful progression, but we can place the hammer in the hands of the One who cares for us with an everlasting love. Don't just accept the blows of life, instead receive what is needed and behold the beauty of the result. The hands of God are sure and His intentions are true.

> That the genuineness of your faith, being much more precious than gold that perishes, though it is tested by fire, may be found to praise, honor, and glory at the revelation of Jesus Christ. (1 Peter 1:7)

II

EXPECT(ATIONS)

My soul, wait silently for God alone, for my expectation is from Him.

Psalm 62:5

We expect—look forward to, wait, watch, anticipate, and hope for—certain things during a day, a week, a year, or a lifetime. It is reasonable for us to expect to see a sunrise or sunset, or to eat food and drink water in the course of a day. These met expectations keep us on schedule, allowing for a certain amount of freedom for our minds, bodies, and souls to operate. They preserve the peace within us. Unmet expectations often occur because we have created standards apart from the reality of other people and have built a day, a week, or a life around something that cannot be attained. Frustration, fear, hate, and all sorts of ugliness can boil over from the pot of unmet expectations simmering within us.

There is a very visible discontentment in some people today that is vague and ill-defined. If we have this discontent and it is not addressed, it will weary our life and water down the substance of our existence. We may redefine and reposition ourselves in such a way to escape this restlessness, but we cannot escape the reality that challenges our false perceptions and will always prohibit us from finding the peace that we seek.

You, me, and all of society cannot afford to create a false concept of God. Doing so erects a foundation of standards and conditions that will go unfulfilled. These are unacceptable to God and can never match up to His reality. Mankind's greatest need is God, but the greatest source of mankind's discontentment is the creation of faulty criteria based upon personal preference. These ideals may be good in themselves, but their application will always fluctuate depending upon a person's circumstances. The resulting uncertainty is fake medicine sold by satan as a promised cure all.

I have come to realize that the greatest disappointments originate from trying to engineer outcomes and hoping in preconceived and fabricated ideals. These may all proceed from good intentions but may not be what the Master desires. Look for the purposes He has set in your life. Follow His standards, and place your hope in Him alone. His timing and strength will be revealed to you. It is Who He is, and it is what He does. Let God alone set your expectations.

III

FORGIVENESS

They paid no attention, and Manasseh seduced them to do more evil than the nations whom the LORD had destroyed before the children of Israel.

2 Kings 21:9

God continually amazes me in how He shows us His tremendous mercy by pouring out His love on the life of others. It is even harder to comprehend His mercy toward me.

Take for example the story of Manasseh (see 2 Chronicles 33). He was pure wickedness from the get-go. Destroying all the good his father Hezekiah had done, he introduced all sorts of nastiness into the ritual worship of God, included the sacrificing of his own children! Yet he reigned in Jerusalem for fifty-five years!

Why would God allow such evil to prevail for so long? Perhaps it was to reveal that His absolute mercy and forgiveness is available to all when they call upon on His name. This became evident when at the end of his rope, and the end of his life, Manasseh did turn to God (see 2 Chronicles 33:10-17).

God showed justice to Manasseh by warning and punishing him. Given the nature of Manasseh's rebellion, we are not surprised by God's punishment: Manasseh was defeated and sent into exile at the hands of the Assyrians.

What really stretches our mind is that God granted Manasseh forgiveness when he repented! Manasseh's life was changed. He was given a new start! God's forgiveness made a tremendous impact in his own life, as well as those of all of Israel.

How far are you going to go before crying out to God? How far and how much are you willing to suffer before turning to Him for forgiveness and a new start? The pain and suffering may not go away, but His complete forgiveness will release His eternal life to you in order to keep you capable of looking beyond and above it all!

IV

OUR HUMILITY

By humility and the fear of the LORD are riches and honor and life.

Proverbs 22:4

Andrew Murray wrote: "Pride, or the loss of this humility, is root of every sin and evil."[2]

Pride was cultivated in the Garden of Eden by satan, and then passed on to us through the sin of Adam and Eve. Society infuses pride into our lives through every available marketing outlet shouting out the phrase, "It's all about you!" The Bible teaches that the opposite of this idea is true: *it's not all about you.*

Eternal life is about denying yourself by picking up your cross every day and following Jesus Christ. This command is given in three of the four gospels. The Bible states clearly that in crucifying the flesh (destroying sin) we can live our new life in Christ, which leads to serving others. Jesus said, "For even the Son of Man did not come to be served, but to serve, and to give His life a ransom for many" (Mark 10:45).

Pride (which appeals to the empty head) comes before falling; although, those who fall because of pride will seldom acknowledge that their failure resulted from their own selfish choices.

On the night before His death, Jesus gives His disciples (and, in turn, gives us) the ultimate understanding of how to serve. Taking up a

9

towel, Jesus washed his disciples' feet and told them that a servant cannot be greater than his master. Christ set the example we are to follow. People can be so confused about what God requires of them and how to get to know Him. Worst yet, they may say they are a Christian but do not know the very God they claim to serve!

The Bible, from the beginning to end, describes God's character. It is good to seek to imitate God by consistently humbling ourselves throughout our lives. This can only be accomplished by laying aside any claim to our rights and serving Jesus Christ. He issued the greatest command: "You shall love the LORD your God with all your heart, with all your soul, and with all your mind" (Matthew 22:37).

When left on our own we will continually confirm our selfishness by our own actions. Let us serve Him who gave His all for us and set the perfect example for us to follow.

V

Jesus' Humility

The Son can do nothing of Himself.

John 5:19

In the gospel of John, the inner life of Jesus is revealed. Although the word "humble" is not written, there is no other place in Scripture where His humility is so clearly on display. Examples of Jesus' heart of humility is also discovered in the following Scriptures:

> I can of Myself do nothing. As I hear, I judge; and My judgment is righteous, because I do not seek My own will but the will of the Father who sent Me. (John 5:30)

> I do not receive honor from men. (John 5:41)

> For I have come down from heaven, not to do My own will, but the will of Him who sent Me. (John 6:38)

> Jesus answered them and said, "My doctrine is not Mine, but His who sent Me." (John 7:16)

> ...I have not come of Myself... (John 7:28)

> I do nothing of Myself. (John 8:28)

> ...nor have I come of Myself, but He sent Me... (John 8:42)

> I do not seek My own glory. (John 8:50)

11

The words that I speak to you I do not speak on My own authority; but the Father who dwells in Me does the works. (John 14:10)

...the word which you hear is not Mine but the Father's who sent Me. (John 14:24)

In Christ, we find the Father's will for us—not in doing what we want, but rather in participating in His desires. Jesus did nothing of Himself. He did what His Father desired. In obedience, an individual will discover the power and freedom of the One and only living God.

VI

NEVERLAND

I, brethren, could not speak to you as to spiritual people but as to carnal, as to babes in Christ. I fed you with milk and not with solid food; for until now you were not able to receive it, and even now you are still not able; for you are still carnal. For where there are envy, strife, and divisions among you, are you not carnal and behaving like mere men?

1 Corinthians 3:1-3

On a recent visit to Disneyland, I was relaxing on the Storybook Land ride which is a boat ride that winds through miniature towns from Disney stories. As the boat passed by Neverland, the guide said, "Neverland is a land where Peter Pan lived, and a place where nobody ever grew up." That caused me to think about an apparent contradict-tion: although we are to come to Jesus as a child, Paul tells us that we are to grow in our understanding of Scripture and mature spiritually (see 1 Corinthians 3:1-3). How can we do both?

I love the story of Peter Pan; how he went to London and corralled Wendy and her brothers to accompany him back to Neverland. Pan, Wendy, and all the others had loads of fun and much adventure, but after a time Wendy saw all of it for what it really was. Peter Pan was selfishly stubborn, refusing to grow up and become a mature person who is responsible for his actions.

After the Corinthians converted, the Apostle Paul carefully fed them the basics of the faith (just as a newborn is fed), but these early converts refused to move on to more healthy, solid food. They continued to live carnal, flesh-based, and selfish lives. Although they were saved and recognized Christ as their Lord and Savior, they were not spiritually fit and established in His Word. Instead of seeking the Lord with childlike faith (a faith without preconceived expectations or jaded worldviews), they were acting like children.

There is a progression in our lives when we move from being babes to children to teenagers to adults. Maturity occurs physically, emotionally, and spiritually. It's a process of upward movement that involves learning many lessons, making friends, and eating more solid foods. If we continually drink the milk of babes, we will not mature. The same is true in the body of Christ that can become malnourished just as the Corinthian church was. The spiritual fruit of immaturity includes fighting like children, allowing divisions to distract us, and reacting to our circumstances in the flesh.

I love Disneyland. It really is an escape from reality and the demands of the world, a huge Neverland where adults wear Mickey Mouse ears and everyone gets to be a kid. As much as I would love to live there forever, I know that a life spent in childish behavior of self-centeredness produces zero growth.

Neverland is a great place to visit, but it is where we will end up permanently if we pursue a selfish way of life—never growing in what Jesus died for and never utilizing the gifts He gave to us. I would much rather live my life growing in His grace and the knowledge of Him, eventually residing with My King in that place that is called "Forever Land."

VII

Death & Taxes

As many as received Him, to them He gave the right to become children of God, to those who believe in His name.

John 1:12

Benjamin Franklin said something we've all heard, "In this world nothing can be said to be certain, except death and taxes." No matter how hard we try, we cannot work our way around these two inevitabilities. Unfortunately, this year I experienced them more personally than ever before. My father-in-law died very suddenly and I paid my taxes upon returning home from his funeral.

Few of us want to acknowledge death, much less discuss it. For the most part, it is ugly in nature, associated with disease and suffering, and produces much grief. We tolerate taxes, complain about them, pay them, and wonder how much we truly receive in return. For the Christian, though, death is life—the gateway into eternity; leading to a new, resurrected life in the presence of the Father; free of pain and suffering. However, this new life will not be experienced by all.

The word gospel means "good news." The gospel is good news because it is the message of Jesus Christ, His death on the cross, and His resurrection from the dead. Whoever believes this will pass from life on earth to eternal life with God our Father in heaven. It is also good news that our death here on earth will free us from such burdensome tasks as paying taxes, suffering through disease, and experiencing pain and sorrow. Sadly, so many people complicate this path to heaven by creating man-made doctrines that obscure the entry point.

When you stand before God, He will not ask you what denomination you were. However, He will ask, "Have you accepted My Son as your Lord and Savior?" This is because all who deny Christ will be denied access to heaven (Acts 14:6).

When death strikes a blow that touches you personally, it puts a burden on your heart to share the gospel with others. Without the knowledge of the good news, this very short time on earth is all people have to live for. Search your heart and ask Jesus into it today.

VIII

STRENGTH

Every word of God is pure; He is a shield to those who put their trust in Him.

Proverbs 30:5

While visiting my native state of Wisconsin, several things recaptured my attention: the green of the trees, the waving of the field crops with the wind, the smell of the first cut of hay, and the striking flatness of the land. I took each of these for granted while growing up. I realized the same is true for those people in our lives who are familiar to us—friends and family. We talk to them and see them often. An extended absence can increase our bond, yet unfortunately, many of these relationships are treated as if they will last forever.

We move very quickly through life, seeing many people and things countless times, including those who are close to us. Busyness makes it easy to shift our focus onto me, myself, and I and more often than not, we begin to draw our strength from this "Unholy Trinity."

Unfortunately, sin impacts this world every moment and we are often confronted with situations that make absolutely no sense nor have any answer. Limited by our human nature, we reach out to God to get answers and ask Him to set things aright.

Strength

God tells us to "Be strong and of good courage, do not fear nor be afraid of them; for the LORD your God, He is the One who goes with you. He will not leave you nor forsake you" (Deuteronomy 31:6).

Lately I have been confronted with the death of my father-in-law as well as cancer striking many who are close to me. Accidents, divorce, and age change our familiar landscapes and make us stop to evaluate what we consider important in our lives—not only what we see as noteworthy but who we value as significant.

The world we see and experience is not the world God intended us to live in. Sin has invaded this planet due to the act of Adam and Eve in the garden of Eden. It may not seem fair that we are subject to their decision, but "all have sinned and fall short of the glory of God" (Romans 3:23). God sent his only Son to die on the cross for us so that we can live in eternity with Him. However, the same God who died for us also gave us the free will to choose whom we will serve. Who or what we serve determines the source of our strength.

It is easy to become defeated in this world. It is not a perfect place, but when we draw from His strength, He provides us with the courage to not fear. God informs us that His ways are not our ways, His thoughts are not our thoughts, and it is not for us to have the knowledge of all things (see Isaiah 55:8). It is enough to only know the One Who has that knowledge. There are so many vibrant green fields filled with healthy crops and a whole lot of life in this world. There is more abundance available to us when we draw our strength to live and to love from Him.

IX

THE THINGS WE DO

He said to them all, "If anyone desires to come after Me, let him deny himself, and take up his cross daily, and follow Me."

Luke 9:23

Let's face it. We all enjoy doing the things we like to do when we want to do them, while kicking back and pleasing ourselves in the process. Even if these situations don't work out as planned, it doesn't deter us from doing the same things again in the future. It's no surprise that our desire for pleasurable down time increases when it seems to be beyond our reach. We become cranky and edgy when these moments of enjoyment are few and far between.

God is working on me in this area. He has put me in places and situations where, for weeks at a time, my attention focuses on others rather than myself. I've been far from home with spotty internet service, in different beds, reading random devotions and Bible passages. Some days found me doing exhausting labor that demanded the very last bit of my strength.

For the most part, I did okay; although, there were days when my flesh cried out demanding to end what was required of me. What kept me going? I held fast to the promises of God while remembering that there is no greater privilege than serving Jesus Christ.

In the days Jesus walked the earth, "taking up one's cross" meant a very painful death. He tells us to take up our own cross, not His, every single day (see Luke 9:23). Most of us can't grasp this because we don't like being told what to do. However, the realization of what is right is revealed in the holding and carrying our cross.

It is hard to die to self. Yet, it is the only way to make our biggest impact for Jesus. We are to be the best, strongest, most well-equipped Christians we can be. It is when our soul and heart have been laid open by whatever baffling circumstances life throws at us—things we can never comprehend—that we gain the perfect position to be used mightily by God.

As God works on me, it hurts because there are certain "me-myself-and-I" things that I would really like to have, but God is the Master Planner, as well as the Master Potter, who shapes and forms me for His good work. The process can be painful, both inside and out. Although it hurts in the middle of the circumstances, I know that good spiritual fruit and access to strength beyond measure will be waiting for me when it's over.

Those who believe in Jesus Christ can grab onto these truths to help them engage in the Father's business. If you don't know Jesus personally, then simply tell Him that you devote your life to Him right now. In this way, you won't miss out on being able to live a life full of strength beyond measure. (The eternal benefits aren't bad either.)

X

REMINDER

For this reason I will not be negligent to remind you always of these things [faith, virtue, knowledge, self-control, perseverance, godliness, brotherly kindness and love], though you know and are established in the present truth. Yes, I think it is right, as long as I am in this tent, to stir you up by reminding you, knowing that shortly I must put off my tent, just as our Lord Jesus Christ showed me. Moreover I will be careful to ensure that you always have a reminder of these things after my decease.

2 Peter 1:12-15 (items in brackets added)

The other day I went for a bicycle ride. No big deal, although over the past several weeks I had been getting out a bit more and felt as though my legs were stronger. I chose to ride a route which I had only done once before. It was more miles than my usual routes and contained many climbs: three of which were very steep and others that were long. The ride out wasn't too bad, but coming back over those small mountains caused my legs to ache and my heart to pound as if it was going to jump right out of my chest!

Now, I know how to ride a bike, and I knew what was in store for me, but yet it was easy to overestimate my own strength and endurance. The same can also occur in our Christian walk as we go through life. We take comfort in thinking that there is great security in many years of walking with the Lord: going to church innumerable times, reading

21

the Bible from time to time, and praying occasionally. We sense our own strength in these activities and don't need anyone telling us much more about anything. At this point, we have set ourselves up for a fall.

Peter was at the end of his life when he wrote the two letters that bear his name. He tells the church that as long as he is drawing breath, he is going to keep reminding them of the same things over and over and over again. Why? Because we all tend to forget the things we need to remember and remember the things we need to forget! We need to be constantly reminded of what is essential and what God wants to do with us.

Paul tells us in 1 Corinthians 10:12, "Therefore let him who thinks he stands take heed lest he fall." We need to be careful of exactly what Paul is getting at here. You see, we are very good at overestimating our own abilities, while at the same time underestimating, and even putting down, the abilities of those around us. This makes us feel and look better. Although this pride seems like a small thing, it is the very sin that took satan down.

Be it riding steep hills on a bike ride or living through the tough times of life, we need these difficulties to reveal our physical and spiritual strength. I am pushing through in both of these areas because either the ultimate goal is farther away than I originally thought or maybe my perspective has changed. The race route can look short from a spectator's view, but the participant knows the true length of those grueling miles.

We should always remember that while we are dealing with life's steep slopes, sharp curves, and dead ends, we are becoming stronger and stronger. When we sit and do little to nothing, we end up getting weak and begin to retreat. Building strength through praying continually, reading His Word and obeying His commandments (and exercising!) will allow us to climb whatever mountains lie in our path!

XI

THE MIDDLE

Therefore, beloved brethren, be steadfast, immovable, always abounding in the work of the Lord, knowing that your labor is not in vain in the Lord.

1 Corinthians 15:58

While playing, watching, and coaching baseball, I have come to realize something about the game. A little understood insight into the great American pastime is that the winner or loser of the game is often determined by how the game is played during the middle innings. We can profit from this idea in our living as Christians. For instance, during the "middle innings" of our trials, ministry, or life in general, it is vitally important that we don't lose heart, or become complacent. It is our reaction during these times that will often determine the outcome of our life.

The Apostle Paul gives us this great advice, "Let us not grow weary while doing good, for in due season we shall reap if we do not lose heart" (Gal 6:9). Our human nature causes us to desire new things and to be entertained by something original, different, unique, or exciting. We often struggle with maintaining diligence throughout the more monotonous activities of our daily lives. Paul was telling the Galatians to not be discouraged and to continue doing what is right, even if they didn't see immediate tangible results. Paul's encouragement to the Galatians still applies today as we need to keep doing good and trusting God for the results. In due time, we will reap a harvest of blessing.

Right now, God may have you doing something that may seem like a real drag. It may not be producing the fruit you expect, and you may feel like you are getting pummeled by the world. The truth continues to be that if God has called you to a certain place or ministry, then you are to stand fast and not grow weary, particularly if the task is only halfway done—if you are still in the middle of the game.

It's how we participate in the middle that will determine the outcome of the game. Our execution, obedience, attitude, and strength must not only be worked out with diligence at the beginning, but most importantly in the middle. This is where most people get tired, where it begins to seem that nobody is looking, and that few are concerned. This, though, is the time when victory is most often won or lost.

Being just over half-way done with my Bible college studies, I find myself from time to time thinking of what I will be doing a year now. However, instead of entertaining those thoughts, I become more determined to get as close to Jesus as possible. I stay in the game by warding off distractions. I let Him open my eyes by reading His words, seeing His promises, His strength, and His compassion toward me. If you feel like you are in a bit of a "slump," I encourage you to take a few extra "swings" in God's "batting cage"—read the Bible to see how much better equipped you are by standing in His strength and not growing weary in the middle innings of life. It will refresh you to finish the game as a winner.

XII

THANKSGIVING

Enter into His gates with thanksgiving, and into His courts with praise.
Be thankful to Him and bless His name.

Psalm 100:4

It's always a perfect time to remember what we have to be thankful for.

GOD - This must be first and foremost on all our lists of thankfulness. Job said, "I have heard of You by the hearing of the ear, but now my eye sees You" (Job 42:5). Let's just not pretend to know Him; instead let's seek to understand who God really is by hearing and seeing Him.

FAMILY - I love spending time with my family. Our time together is usually gone all too quickly, and we are unable to ever get back a wasted day.

THE BIBLE THAT CONTAINS GOD'S PROMISES - The Bible contains all of God's promises. Life is uncertain; God's promises are not because He cannot lie (see Titus 1:2). The promises of God will get us through life when life is not through with us.

OPTIMISM - My glass is half full. How about yours? "Bless the LORD, O my soul; and forget not all His benefits" (Psalm 103:2).

THE SIMPLE THINGS IN LIFE - Here are just a few: Sunday night meals of cheese, popcorn, crackers, and apples; naps, hugs, and high fives; someone coming to know Christ; an encouraging smile. Life isn't that complicated—we just make it that way. Keep your life uncluttered and you will see much more.

CELEBRATING THE LITTLE THINGS - After eleven years, I hit the 5,000-mile mark on my bicycle! My family and I enjoyed a celebration lunch.

STOP AND SMELL THE ROSES - I did this last week. The roses on the Bible college campus were so incredibly colorful and fragrant that I had to be completely into myself not to stop and notice! It wasn't so much the awesome fragrance, as it was the unforgettably deep colors that got my attention: yellows and reds so profound that the roses didn't appear to be real.

FRIENDS - I love my friends and hold them close to my heart. Let's all be a better friend and make more of them.

PRAYER - Develop the practice of prayer and do it daily. It's a breath when needed and hope realized.

FREEDOM - Never forget the men and women who gave, and continue to give, their lives for this country.

Let us develop a heart that is forever thankful!

XIII

BROKEN HEART

I have heard of You by the hearing of the ear, but now my eye sees You.

Job 42:5

Some events during the course of our lives change us forever. These can include: graduating from high school and/or college, getting married, having kids, accepting Jesus as Lord and Savior, and going on a mission trip. That last item might possibly be the most life changing. I'd like to encourage anyone who hasn't been on a mission trip to go on one. In the simplicity, hardship, joy, and setbacks of any mission-oriented trip, God is always there to guide you. He will direct you and, most importantly, break your heart for the people you are serving in order to do a work in your life that will be everlasting.

On a recent trip I took to the country of Colombia in Central America, God broke down many of my false beliefs about Him. Most notably, I let Him tear down my walls that prevented the Almighty Ancient of Days from working on my behalf. I had good general ideas about God's character, but it wasn't until I saw how He transcends all lines of race, language, and economic standing to use all kinds of people when they are available to Him that I realized how low my view of Him was.

Grabbing my heart in Colombia and breaking it wide open, God was able to sow his love, grace, and mercy into me. He tore down the barriers that defined who I thought He was and destroyed my perceptions of how He operated. I then willingly submitted to His work, whatever that was going to be. I discovered a tremendous blessing when the children in Santo Domingo (the poorest of poor communities) put their dirty hands in mine. All they wanted was to have someone love them just for a moment. I placed my hand into theirs, looking past the dirt and filth that covered their bodies and saw them as God does.

We are no different than these children when we are living a life without Jesus. We are dirty, grimy, smelly, full of sin, and we will remain this way until our hearts and lives are willing to accept Jesus as Lord, the ruler of our lives. Jesus is willing to reach out to us while we are in this condition, a state that if unchanged condemns us to an eternity spent apart from God, not in heaven, but living in the Lake of Fire.

In holding those little hands, full of filth, and giving countless piggy-back rides to dirty and unkempt children, I simply extended the love the Father poured into my open heart; a love that I could not have generated on my own. Jesus wants to do the same work in all our lives, but we must give ourselves first to Him and let the God of the universe go to work. Don't fence Him in or sell Him short, but instead, be ready to have your heart broken so that He can change you forever.

XIV

KNOWING HIM

The people who know their God shall be strong and carry out great exploits.

Daniel 11:32

From the time I first wrote this until the time you read it, many Resurrection Sunday's will have come and gone. Among all the colored eggs, the chocolate bunnies, jellybeans (my favorite food), and pretty dresses, I hope you can still find what the celebration is all about. Although the risen Christ is celebrated on this day, we carry the significance of this event through every day of the year. We need to remember that His tomb is empty. We serve a God who is very real and alive.

The key to withstanding the storms that life brings (and I guarantee you, those storms will come) is trusting and obeying the living God. This trust is developed, as the prophet Daniel tells us, by knowing God (see Daniel 11:32). How is this done? Trust is built as we grow in our understanding, recognition, and experience of God. He never hides Himself from the world. He can be seen in creation, in the complexity of the human body, and of course most importantly, in the Bible.

The Apostle Paul said, "I determined not to know anything among you except Jesus Christ and Him crucified" (1 Corinthians 2:2). Paul began where we all need to begin: by setting our sights above, looking beyond the obvious, and recognizing God in the midst of every encounter of our lives. He isn't limited to what we can think or do, but rather can do anything He pleases (see Luke 1:37). Once we start to understand His nature, we will become stronger and ready to carry out great exploits just like Daniel did.

Then comes the most exciting and thrilling part of a Christian life—living it out. When you truly believe in something, when you are sold out for it, you will want to do it whole heartedly. Not only will you grow you in your relationship with Christ, you will model His life for others to see.

Seek Jesus Christ throughout the entire year, and get to know Him. Spend time in His Word every day because God will reveal Himself to you there. Godly strength and character are developed in His presence. The more you spend time with Him, the more you will begin to understand Him, recognize Him, and truly experience all He has for you. Jesus Christ completely sold Himself out for you on the cross. He is completely committed to His creation, but His grace can only be offered and is never forced. You must want to receive it. "Do not be afraid; only believe" (Mark 5:36).

XV

PROMISES

To you it has been granted on behalf of Christ, not only to believe in Him, but also to suffer for His sake.

Philippians 1:29

The promises and blessings of God are numerous, but on this earth, suffering will come along with eternal life. It is in the best interest of all believers to pay attention not only to this verse but also to other verses that speak of persecution. We need to develop a mindset that is prepared for pain, as well as looking for the benefits of enduring through it when it comes, for the benefits of suffering are found with the anguish. There four benefits that come to my mind.

First, suffering takes your eyes off earthly comforts. The prophet Habakkuk stood in his tower and asked God, "Why all the suffering?"

He did what we so often do when in crisis, pain, or dilemma: he became self-focused and lost his ability to see where God was positioned in the situation. Seeing his problem from the Almighty God's perspective finally comforted him.

Second, suffering weeds out superficial believers. Once again, we look at the prophet who said, "The just shall live by his faith" (Habakkuk 2:4). This isn't the faith of a pastor, the guy next door, nor your parents' faith. You will have to live according to your own faith. Suffering gives you a clear choice—turn to God or turn away from

Him. When you go to Him, you get to know the Almighty, and your relationship with Him becomes stronger. Rely on His strength, and through suffering you will build your own faith!

Third, suffering strengthens those who endure. While watching the Tour de France this year, I heard the commentators make a statement that the "mountains were making the cyclists suffer." These riders went into the race knowing they would need to endure pain— unbelievable physical agony and discomfort. Yet each rider had developed a mindset of knowing the difficulty that lay ahead, and then prepared for it. In a similar way, through the process and pain of our suffering, Jesus can become very real to us. It is in these times that we need to learn who He is and become perfected through the process of adversity.

Fourth, suffering reveals the One we are following to those who are watching us. Those in search of the meaning of life need to witness suffering in the life of a Christian. They need to see a believer whose eyes are continually on Christ, not self, and becoming stronger in the process of pain. They need to see a believer who knows what is occurring and isn't surprised by it or anxious about it. When the world witnesses faith in action, they will be drawn to Him.

Christ knew it was the will of the Father to suffer by taking on the sins of the entire world. We should not be taken by surprise when adversity strikes us. Do not ask to be immediately delivered from it, but rather ask God how He might be glorified through it. For someone who has not asked Jesus into their life, this process of suffering is dreadful, fearful, and seemingly without purpose. In Christ, we can always have the peace and declare as Habakkuk did, "Yet I will rejoice in the LORD, I will joy in the God of my salvation" (Habakkuk. 3:18).

XVI

HOPE

Let us hold fast the confession of our hope without wavering, for He who promised is faithful.

Hebrews 10:23

There are two different kinds of hope in this life. The hope of the world can be understood as a feeling of expectation, a desire for a certain thing to occur. The hope the Bible speaks of is defined as knowing God and resting in His love. This hope places all burdens, cares, and desires into God's hands. Each of us go through life daily placing our hope in so many different things: a car, food, or the weather. At first glimpse, these objects may appear to be beneficial, but they offer little substance concerning knowledge and rest in God.

The hope of the world puts all reliance upon people or situations. This hope may start to waiver when there is a loss, a move, or a different job. It is during these times that our actions show what we believe in most strongly. The hope of the world, apart from Christ, will leave us empty, broken, and searching. The hope of the Bible is found in Jesus Christ. This hope fulfills, completes, and releases to a person the power of the resurrection and eternal life that extends well beyond this world.

One of the saddest verses in the Bible to me is found in Numbers. It is the attitude of the Israelites right before they reached the Promised

Land. Three of the twelve tribes told Moses, "Do not take us over the Jordon" (Numbers 32:5). The Promised Land, known as "the land of milk and honey," lay on the other side of the Jordon river. It was a gift to them from God Himself. Yet they decided to settle for less, falling short of the fulfillment of God's promise to occupy the land by selling out the future He had for them. They allowed their own fear to dash the hope that God had waiting for them.

When an individual puts their hope in the world, the result is less than God's best and the outcome is separation from the promises God wants to release to us. When we place our hope in Christ, we begin to see with His eyes. The assurance of eternity becomes permanently etched into our hearts and our minds. We will no longer see problems as obstacles, but rather as food to eat that gives us the power to conquer the territory promised to us (see Numbers 14:9).

Don't be like the three tribes of Israel that settled for less. Place all your hope in the Lord and see how He will bring you to what He has promised.

XVII

TIME TO SEE GOD

To everything there is a season, a time for every purpose under heaven.

Ecclesiastes 3:1

Time is not only limited, it also moves quickly. We tend to forget that we are given a limited amount of it to live, and yet we get to spend it however we please. A year can be broken down as follows: 365 days or 8,700 hours or 525,600 minutes or 31,536,000 seconds. It doesn't matter how it's quantified; it all comes out the same.

We must remember that yesterday is forever gone, and we are not promised tomorrow. Are we to enter each day with a fatalistic attitude? No. But we must realize that time can easily escape our attention and cannot be taken back. That's why it's important to realize how we spend our time: for good or for evil.

It is much more difficult to see God's presence when we engage in unforgiveness, hatred, bitterness, or any other sin. We can be very good at justifying the things we do, but don't be fooled—if our time is not spent for God, who is it spent for? Remember, that while living on this earth we either spend time wisely or we waste it.

Jesus Christ is the same yesterday, today, and forever (see Hebrews 13:8). The truth is that we are not. We are constantly changing. He created us with a purpose, He loves us, and He desires for us to come to Him. But He will not force us to do anything we do not want to.

Although we've been granted life on earth, our time is limited. Whereas, the time we will spend in eternity is unlimited.

Let's live within God's powerful purpose for us and be wise stewards of our time. Jesus Christ puts everything into proper perspective. He puts pain, problems, and all our questions into perfect order and peace. I will not get all my questions answered here on earth, but I know when my time comes that everything will be in harmony. So please take the time to see God today. As you lift your eyes up to Him, you will be amazed at how wonderful things look!

XVIII

THIS SAME JESUS

"Men of Galilee, why do you stand gazing up into heaven? This same Jesus, who was taken up from you into heaven, will so come in like manner as you saw Him go into heaven."

Acts 1:11

In the verse above, the apostles were looking up to heaven as Jesus ascended to be seated at the right hand of the Father. Maybe they were thinking that the resurrected Christ, who had walked among them for the past forty days, was now gone again and not coming back. The things they once knew, the daily instruction and comfort Jesus had provided, now appeared lost forever.

The angel reassured them that the same Jesus who had just left them to go to heaven would come back in the same way. Jesus stated, "Nevertheless I tell you the truth. It is to your advantage that I go away; for if I do not go away, the Helper will not come to you; but if I depart, I will send Him to you" (John 16:7). Who is this Helper? It is none other than the Holy Spirit, the third Person of the Godhead (aka the Trinity). Jesus did not leave us alone. He sent His own Spirit to dwell within us, to provide us with strength for each day, and to give us the ability to do things that we could never do by ourselves.

Sometimes we forget this promise and try to tackle all that comes our way by ourselves in our own abilities. The road ahead seems perilous to us so we try to find another way, only to discover that none exists. We become fearful, anxious, and lose sight of what we have come to know about who our God really is.

Jesus said, "I will never leave you nor forsake you" (Hebrews 13:5). If we persist in looking around for something other than what we have already been given, we will easily forget the promises and power of God. Once we are able to comprehend His ascension and ultimate return, we will gain the ability to remember His promises and peacefully persevere through such times as we are in. If you have never accepted Jesus Christ as Lord and Savior, now is the time. And if you have—start believing!

XIX

REFRESHING

Come to Me, all you who labor and are heavy laden, and I will give you rest.

Matthew 11:28

Let's face it, life can be a grind and seem endless at times. We go from task to task, take our kids here and there, getting caught up in an endless cycle of living. Life itself can become dull, gray, and eventually meaningless. We dread Mondays, lift our heads on "hump day," and praise the weekend, only to be cycled back through this routine fifty-one more times a year. It is when we are feeling this way that we need to hear Jesus whispering to us, "Come to Me and I will give you rest" (Matthew 11:28).

It is easy to forget to sustain our spiritual habits when we are worn down physically. Although our spiritual being is much more important than our physical body, it is often ignored. We eat, get a little exercise, and sleep every night, but spiritually we are starving, unfit, and far from rest. We often put aside the most important activities of spiritual discipline. Yet, when we come to Jesus, He not only gives us rest, He fills us and provides us with an absolutely unshakable meaning to life, both now and forever!

In Him, we no longer live for the weekend but can rest in His presence in the midst of the grind. As we learn to come to Him, for rest and refreshment, we will receive the respite that He always freely provides. In coming to Him, we will be refreshed, we will gain strength, and we will rise up above the grind. "Those who wait on the LORD shall renew their strength; they shall mount up with wings like eagles, they shall run and not be weary, they shall walk and not faint" (Isaiah 40:31).

Walking, running, resting, and learning can all be done in and through Jesus, but we need to come to Him. If there is something stopping you from doing this, you must address it immediately! Our tendency as mere humans is to try and tackle our problems ourselves, but this only fills our lives with struggle, turmoil, and self-doubt. The world likes to tell us: "I'm okay, you're okay." The reality is: "Jesus is okay. I'm a mess!"

The rest Jesus promises includes His love, His healing, and peace. Relationship with Jesus changes meaningless, wearisome toil into spiritually productive purpose. We don't just live for living's sake and then die when it is all over. There is a reason to live! If we deny His rest, we will live in self-doubt and think that life doesn't amount to much. Instead, we need faith in Christ and God at the center of our life.

XX

DAD

The only thing that walks back from the tomb with the mourners and refuses to be buried is the character of a man. This is true. What a man is, survives him. It can never be buried.[3]

J.R. Miller

My father passed away on May 18, 2009. Although it did not come as a surprise, Art Jagemann will surely be missed by many and remembered always. As the quote above states, you can't bury the character or qualities distinctive to an individual. My father was a "character"—fun, full of love, and giving—yet, he did much of it under the radar. Oh, he will by no means be ready to be declared a saint, but who is? I can say without any hesitation that he was a great dad. I would not have wanted any other.

I count myself doubly blessed. Along with the best earthly father a person could have, I am also blessed with a great heavenly Father. This is because I believe in His son, Jesus Christ, and confess Him to be my Lord and Savior. This makes me a part of the body of Christ. You can do the same and also be blessed with an exceptional heavenly Father.

It's ironic, but in the sermon I preached the day before my dad died, I used his name as an acronym for the definition of a believer in Christ:

Dad

A - Adhere to Christ

R - Rely on Christ

T - Trust in Christ

I believed in my earthly dad just as much as my heavenly one; I adhered to, relied on, and trusted in him. He was awesome, and through his character he has touched many lives. His impact will survive for many generations to come.

Once, while visiting my dad, he wanted me to try on four pairs of his cowboy boots because he could not wear them anymore. Lining them up, I began to try them on. The first two were size nine-and-a-half, pointed on the toe, and a bit tight on me. The next pair were a thing of beauty, now my favorite, size ten and a perfect fit! The last pair, a ten-and-a-half, were clearly his favorite due to the appearance of having many miles on them. I put them on, trying to convince myself they fit, but it didn't work, no matter how many pairs of socks I wore.

The last pair of my dad's boots may not have fit, but the lessons they spoke of had nothing to do with wearing, but learning. Becoming a better man every day and growing in his relationships is what my dad did—living, learning, and quietly teaching others what he knew. He was a character, he was good, he was my dad.

XXI

BELIEVE

He [Abraham] believed in the LORD, and He accounted it to him for righteousness.

Genesis. 15:6

The word *believe* is often misquoted, misused, and abused. It is one of the most misplaced, degraded, and tarnished words in the English language. I used to *believe* in things such as: Santa, evolution, my invincibility, and many more things along these same lines. In Hebrew *believe* means to establish or to confirm. Abraham truly *believed* (was established and confirmed) in God, and for that he lived from blessing to blessing.

Too often we make the mistake of saying we *believe* in something, only to find out that when the rubber hits the road, we head for the nearest exit. As a Christian, we are to exercise our belief in Christ, not leave that belief deflated outside of Him. God does not give us an over-coming life; He gives us life as we overcome. This life is the result of truly believing all He tells us in the Bible.

While moving about on this planet we will be shaken, stirred, and poured out. I was not put here to work all my life, retire exhausted, and then die. Instead, I *believe* (I am truly sustained and supported with deep roots) that Jesus Christ died, was buried, and rose again for me. I believe He forgives all my sins, so that I can live full of blessings in fellowship with Him as My Creator Lord, not needing to live a life full of toil.

Life takes on a much deeper meaning when you realize that what you believe does in fact exist. For instance, I believe that when physical death overcomes me, I will immediately be in the presence of the Lord.

Abraham had nothing but promises, but those assurances came from the Almighty God. Believing in what God had told him, he followed His lead, even though he never attained those promises. We get the wrong idea of God when we expect His promises to come to pass immediately and for them to include blessings upon blessings. His blessings are indeed plentiful: "Blessed be the Lord, who daily loadeth us with benefits, even the God of our salvation. Selah." (Psalm 68:19 KJV), but God is more concerned with the process of developing our belief in Him than He is in our comfort.

God never gives us strength for tomorrow, or even the next hour, but only for the strain of the moment. It is through this that we suddenly become so rooted in Him, trusting in Him, that nothing—nothing—can or will move us away from Him. Believe in Christ! That is the meaning of life!

XXII

BEGINNING BY THE BASICS

Who are You, Lord? Lord, what do You want me to do?

Acts 9:5-6

Questions, questions, questions. It seems as if there are always so many things to look at, review, edit, compute, or decide. Sometimes it would be nice to block everything out, or better yet, answer the demands with more questions. Whether they are good questions or bad, each offers the opportunity for a new beginning. Brief, deep, and possibly life changing decisions often determine not only who you follow but also why.

Saul, who later became the apostle Paul, was persecuting Christians, throwing as many of them as he could into jail. On his way to Damascus, God knocked him down. Saul then asked two very important questions: "Who are you Lord?" and "What do you want me to do?" These questions form the beginning of the basics, while at the same time, pursue an unknown end. Beginnings offer many things: newness, hope and freshness. Yet, these can soon be forgotten when the present day becomes the past and unfulfilled dreams lie in piles of paperwork, chores, and errands where they eventually die. Life can quickly become something less than what we'd hoped for. Saul was experiencing this.

Being full of zeal, Saul persecuted those whom he thought were the enemies of the Jewish religion. He had lost track of the purpose of his

Jewish roots and all that they promised, including the Messiah. Then, that very Messiah broke into Saul's life and he asked, "Who are you Lord?" All of life stood still. Saul quickly accepted Jesus as His Savior, never looking back and never counting the cost of what he left behind. He learned about God and gave Him both honor and glory. This led him to ask what many people have since asked: "Lord, what do You want me to do?"

We often draw up a huge plan, put things all in order, and then watch as that plan falls apart. Nothing appears to go right—the seams rip, the dam breaks, and we cry out to God, "What's going on?" Just as Jesus directed Saul, He wants to direct our lives one step at a time. For this to happen we must first pursue Him and find out who He really is, not who we think He is. Second, we must ask Him what He wants us to do. It is only through this process that all of life begins to make some sense.

XXIII

SUCCESS!

If the ax is dull, and one does not sharpen the edge, then he must use more strength; but wisdom brings success.

Ecclesiastes 10:10

We all, either consciously or subconsciously, strive to be successful. Sometimes, this can be as simple as hitting a baseball, sinking a putt, finishing a sermon, making it through survival camp, or the granddaddy of them all, getting your kids to clean their room! The masses of people are very relentless in their pursuit of comfort, luxury, and what is deemed as "success." God sets different instructions on how success is understood. A good starting point can be found in the instructions God gave Joshua as he prepared to cross over into the Promised Land.

"Be strong and of good courage...Only be strong and very courageous" (Joshua 1:6-7). Not only were these words of encouragement for Joshua, they were directly from the Lord Himself. Before hearing these words, he had studied, watched, and worked under Moses during the previous forty years in the desert. Joshua saw the miracles God did through Moses in Egypt, at the Red Sea, and in the desert. Joshua also helped to win numerous battles, so in the eyes of many he was already a success. When he succeeded Moses as the leader of the children of Israel, why do you think God told him to be strong and courageous on five different occasions?

Success!

In a word, the answer is "freshness." These fresh words of encouragement reminded Joshua just exactly where his strength and success came from. It wasn't from his own smarts, schemes, battle plans, or hefty 401k. No, it came from realizing God's will for him. He didn't hesitate to do what God desired. To go all out for God was already his greatest passion. This is the unfailing prerequisite of eternal success.

God continued to let Joshua know in verses six through eight that he shouldn't turn to the left or right of the law, and to meditate on the Word constantly. God promised him that if he did this, "then you will have good success" (v.8). The world throws curves at us. We will experience hardship, but if we are in God's Word it is easier to realize that we are in the only place that will offer the strength and courage that leads to success.

In order to succeed, God must define our success. We can be encouraged, through the life of Joshua, to receive a new freshness. By the words of God, we are reminded where to store our treasures and look for victory. The pursuit for success may differ for many, but we can learn to appreciate God speaking and strengthening us daily through His Word. Now that is a recipe for success and something you can only accomplish with Jesus Christ as your Lord and Savior!

XXIV

TOUR DE TRUST

Blessed are all those who put their trust in Him.

Psalm 2:12

One of the most grueling sporting events in the entire world runs for three weeks in July. This isn't the NFL draft or me trying to play eighteen holes of golf. It is the Tour de France, which is roughly 2,100 gut wrenching miles of bicycle racing with mountains, crazy crowds, cobblestone roads, and lots of saddle sores. I cannot fathom the pain, suffering, and exhaustion that these athletes endure.

It may not be the Tour de France or the miles involved, but daily living involves trust—what we put ourselves through as well as who and what we place our trust in. This small word *put* carries a lot of weight. For example, we can talk and act like we trust in someone or something, but it is not until we *put* value into it that our actions fulfill our words. I might think an investment is a good one, but it is not until I *put* my own money down that I exhibit trust. What's truly amazing is that we so willingly put our money, futures, safety, and eternal security in things that are so temporary, untested, and downright evil.

The riders on the Tour de France put their lives in the hands of mechanics, team leaders, and the peloton (the main group of riders). During the race, crashes occur, road rashes hurt, and many riders will drop out and be disappointed. Life is no different as we continually and without much thought, put our trust in our cars, the drivers around us, leaders, and countless other things.

Those who go through life without any relationship with Jesus Christ are putting their eternal security into something that is fleeting, and when life feels like the endless grind of the Tour, the only satisfactory solution seems to be a quick exit. A Christian is never promised a relaxed ride or a short and flat stretch of road. However, we have the assurance of knowing that this race, our life, will end one day full of blessings in realizing that we have put our trust in Him.

There are those who talk a good game, but until they get out and do something their talk is meaningless. C.S. Lewis made a great observation when he said, "We may think God wants actions of a certain kind, but God wants people of a certain kind."[4] What kind of people does He want? Those who humbly come to Him and put their entire life into His hands saying, "Here I am!" Actions are meaningless and self-serving unless they are placed at the feet of Jesus. Be a mighty person of God and give it all to Him today!

XXV

THE FIGHT

Eleazar stood up and struck down the Philistines until his hand was weary and clung to the sword.

2 Samuel 23:10 (AMP)

An acquaintance of mine recently told me his brother was tired of fighting; that as he was getting older, the battles and issues of life were just not worth his time or effort. He was satisfied by only doing what needed to be done. Looking at each other, we both agreed not to ever do this; that no matter what worthy issue came along, we would be ready and willing to go to battle for the Lord. This is always much easier said than done, especially when you aren't knee deep in bedlam, bills, and health issues. However, this is where God currently has me and is using me. By looking upon Him, I find complete and perfect peace and the strength of the Almighty.

King David had thirty mighty men who followed, served, and loved him. Eleazar was one of those men. In one battle he fought so long, and so hard, that by the end of the battle, although he was completely exhausted, he could not release his sword. What drove this man to such great exploits? It was his complete devotion to a man (David) who was totally sold-out to God.

Faith in God is not some weak and pitiful excursion, but is a strong and vigorous confidence built on the fact that it is in Christ that complete revelation for all that matters is found. I am only one man, who can and will fail, but I will hopefully never lose a grip on the calling of Christ upon my life. Let us be an example to the masses and show to them Jesus during our troubles and that He alone is in the fight and worthy of it.

XXVI

LOOPHOLES

Enter by the narrow gate; for wide is the gate and broad is the way that leads to destruction, and there are many who go in by it. Because narrow is the gate and difficult is the way which leads to life, and there are few who find it.

Matthew 7:13-14

Most likely, tax season is no one's favorite time. It's the time of year when we put together our scraps of paper, receipts, and notes that have been haphazardly squirreled away. A common phenomenon that comes with this event is exploiting loopholes in the tax code. Be it legal or illegal, they are sought out, abused, and, in some cases, flaunted.

In doing the same thing with the Bible, many people seek loopholes in regards to the qualifications necessary for entrance into heaven. Beginning with the first sin in the garden, seeking these loopholes can become a way of life.

A loophole can be described as a means of escape; especially through vagueness or an omission through which obligation may be evaded.

The tax laws of the U.S. government require citizens to pay up. This tax code includes ways of partial escape, some gray areas, much ambiguity, and leaves room for much evasive action. If you fail to pay what is required, you will be fined and possibly have your assets frozen. Unlike the government, God gives us explicit instructions on

53

how to get to heaven. Our obligations are clearly described, nothing is omitted, and definite consequences are attached.

In Matthew 7:13-14, Jesus let the world know the way to eternal life is through the narrow gate. While there are loopholes in the tax laws, there are no escape clauses in His law. Why do people go through life spending so much time frantically justifying what they want to believe and create their own theories? These rationalizations are just straw without any truth, lacking any real strength to pull people through life. People believe in these man-made theories because man wants to be ruled by himself, not God.

You may cheat the government by taking advantage of loopholes in the tax code, but there is absolutely nothing you can do to avoid what comes into every life—death. The tax law has become incredibly complicated, yet since Jesus came, the way to salvation has remained consistently unchanged: "If you confess with your mouth the Lord Jesus and believe in your heart that God has raised Him from the dead, you will be saved" (Romans 10:9).

Don't search for the loophole. Simply give it all to God.

XXVII

THE ITINERARY

There is a way that seems right to a man, but its end is the way of death.

Proverbs 14:12

On a recent trip to Florida, our plans collapsed. Our itinerary had connecting flights from Rapid City to Denver, and then to Tampa. Great plans, good connections, and well—it just didn't happen. Our first flight was delayed for thirty minutes waiting on the crew, but the pilot did make up much of the time in flight. Our hope dwindled as we waited on the Denver runway for the same amount of time since not one of the ninety-five plus gates in the airport were available. Finally, after sprinting from gate ninety-two to gate three, we sadly watched our plane pull away. We were left winded and disappointed, and to make matters worse, I pulled my hip muscle. Many are our best-laid plans, until something occurs to change them.

An itinerary is good to have for a journey since its outlines the when, how, and where of a route. We like to live life based on vague or solid plans of what should take place. Upsetting our schedules can throw us completely off track. Is it really possible to control one's own life? Mind you, I'm not advocating laying back and taking it all as it comes, but rather we need to realize that God is the One who orders our steps (see Psalm 37:24). Living life from this perspective allows us to give the outcomes to Him. When a schedule is disrupted and plans change, peace in these times of uncertainty reside in Him.

While waiting to catch another connecting flight in our nation's capital (Washington, D.C. was not on our original itinerary), I began memorizing a verse written down earlier that morning: "He is before all things, and in Him all things consist" (Colossians 1:17). I sure was not about the "in Him all things consist" part when our airline had been severely lacking in customer service skills. I did, however, find comfort in this verse that God had provided to me. It brought peace and strength as I realized it is God who holds it all together, not me or the airlines.

When I was young, I wanted to be a veterinarian. As I grew older, my interests changed. I have been a landscaper, roofer, two-time business owner, undercover operative, process server, private investigator, substitute teacher, juvenile probation officer, as well as a few other positions. The one thing I never considered becoming was a pastor. That profession was never on my itinerary of life or even an item on my bucket list. Yet, God had a different plan waiting for me as soon as I got on board with Him.

God loves us all so much and has the ultimate travel plan—that all would come to know Jesus Christ as Lord and Savior. This is the plan of redemption from the ultimate catastrophe of hell for which Jesus gave his very own life. It is the ultimate itinerary that leads to everlasting life and the One that will never change. None of us know how many things will be rescheduled in our lives, but if we are in Jesus, we will most definitely live forever with Him. This plan is guaranteed and will never change!

XXVIII

FOCUS!

He [the man who was healed] looked up and said, "I see men like trees, walking." Then He [Jesus] put His hand on his eyes again and made him look up. And he was restored and saw everyone clearly.

Mark 8:24-25

My trip to South Sudan can be summed up as long dusty roads, dirty clothes, lack of sleep, rice and beans (more rice and beans), no electricity, hippos, and sixty eager Army Chaplains from the Sudanese People's Liberation Army who were eagerly awaiting God's Word. Among all these things was a plain truth that God put in my heart: "Keep it simple and live for Me clearly." Despite the rough conditions, it was one of the most blessed times of ministry I have ever experienced because this message kept me focused.

Simplicity and clarity! I love it! It applies to my fashion sense and is the greatest idea since Garanimals. For me, saying, "I am not a slave to fashion, just a victim," means that blue jeans and khakis fill my wardrobe. All kidding aside, this message of simply living the truth proclaimed by God in His Word seems obvious, but in reality it is something of a rarity. The church, in its pursuit of higher learning, has become entangled with the world (which Paul warned against in 2 Timothy 2:3-4), presenting a complicated religion and creating hazy (lazy) Christians.

Focus!

The truth of the Bible convicts us and painfully peels our hearts away to what we are truly made of. A message of uncertainty is not what the world needs to see or hear today. If the Word of God is watered-down, it becomes useless. Complete truth is found only in the Bible and was perfectly modeled by Jesus. The Bible makes us aware that we are sinners in need of a Savior. Accepting this fact is a painful, yet necessary step in receiving Jesus Christ as Lord of our lives.

Along with the message of keeping it simple, Christians need to live a life that gives the world a clear picture of who Jesus is. The world needs to see Jesus, not as a murky mirage, but as a Person who loves, hurts, and stands for absolute truth—as Someone who is real. The world will hate you for displaying your faith. So, don't get into the habit of mixing your own ideas with spiritual truth. It will only keep you in the shallow end of experiencing Jesus.

People tend to merge God's character and His Word into their own image and ideas. My goal is to draw people to God through the truth found in Scripture, then allow the Holy Spirit room to work in their lives. Then, I will get to spend an eternity with them in heaven. If your life is complicated, simply find Jesus and give your entire being to Him. As you live for Him, your life will come into focus.

XXIX

UPSIDE "RIGHT"

These who have turned the world upside down have come here too.

Acts 17:6

Many churches face a problem today. Instead of being the influencer of society, the church has allowed the world to creep in. This has infected the body of Christ, resulting in weak, "fraidy-cat" Christians. Paul and those with him lived distinctively different lives than others around them. Not conforming to the pressures of the society, they based their lives on what Jesus taught them—not to perfection, but to the best of their abilities. These Christians strived to live the life that Jesus required. Unfortunately, many Christians validate man-made worldviews, while using them as the standard for their reality. Doing this cripples the message of what happened on the cross.

Marginalized churches are now hideouts for members only, not meeting places for the hurting and discouraged. This position results in the church being a doormat—trampled upon, taking in all the filth of false teachings—and having many pulpits filled with imposters. If you call yourself a Christian, it is time to turn around and get it right. Never be afraid to declare the truth and to live your life with both feet on the ground—upside "right." Christians are not flawless, but they can live from the spiritual condition of being perfectly loved and completely forgiven.

This world will never be changed by legislating morality. Renewal must be brought about by engaging the culture and letting God do His life changing work one heart at a time. In order to do this, Christians need to be out among the people, living with and loving them. The church cannot stand idly by as a worldly culture leads people astray. We are called to be the salt and light to the world (see Matthew 5:13-16). Satan is a real enemy, a purposeful punk who grabs for our affections, blinds the world to sin, and leads those who fall for his deception to the gates of hell.

The single greatest purpose of the church is not to establish a kingdom here on earth, but to influence people so that they can know that God is real and truly loves them. If you are a Christian, act like one so that those who aren't can know the real Jesus. Christianity is not a behavior modification program. Christianity is not a life manufactured by religion, but rather a life engaged in relationship with Jesus Christ. If your world seems upside down, find the only One who can turn it around. His name is Jesus.

XXX

I'M WITH HIM

For you died, and your life is hidden with Christ in God.

Colossians 3:3

Your identity is directly defined and created by how, where, and who you spend the majority of your time. Whatever you hear or see goes into your heart where you can either accept and digest it or reject and dispose of it. For better or for worse, you are the consumption of all that you do: education, work, relationships, spending resources, and value of life. As a Christian, my greatest strength is found when I look to and lean on God, while realizing all my life comes from Him.

I will never stake a claim to perfection because on my own I will never attain it. Frustration comes easily when we are ship, captain, and crew for our course in life. Lack of success can come from failing to realize that we have inherited a sinful nature from Adam. Although, we can do much good and accomplish many things on our own, we will always feel a huge gulf of emptiness and unworthiness. Why? Because the only One who is able to fill this hole of emptiness is Jesus Christ. We need to surrender control of our life to Jesus and allow Him to set us on the right course. The only way to achieve completeness and strength is to walk with Him and to live for Him.

The mentality of going alone and being a self-made person, will ultimately lead us into major disappointment, as well as personal and spiritual disaster. I speak of this from experience. I do not use God as a crutch, but rather as a body cast for complete protection and support. He makes each day extraordinary by giving me eyes to see those who are hurting. This ability helps me to look beyond myself and realize there is much more to living than what I know.

The new life of being a Christian is an offer to all. It is an invitation to realize that your worth doesn't come from you, but instead from the One who lived and died for everyone. Accepting this offer extinguishes the old you, grants you the grace to live in and with Jesus, and provides you the ability to have life eternally. He will prioritize your life, energize you, and allow you to see that there is a purpose for your life, which is to prepare you for heaven and to bring many people along with you.

XXXI

TIME

My soul follows close behind You; Your right hand upholds me.

Psalm 63:8

There are days, weeks, months, and even years that we would like to skip over, fast- forward through, or erase; but try as we might, we just don't possess that ability. In fact, if we went directly from A to Z and grasped nothing in between, our knowledge, relationships, and life would resemble that of a novel with only one page. Those who don't know Christ are souls adrift, and even some who have committed their lives to Christ are in starvation mode. The point is that the substance of life is formed by giving value to each day.

When we drift through the time apart from God, we have nothing more than a birth date and a death date to define us. Even though some might be influential, without Christ, they will continue to search for the meat and substance of their existence. Hope will always be elusive, and life will continually remain empty.

Christianity is not about going to church, memorizing Bible verses, or taking the title of "Christian" and hanging it on a mantle as if it were some trophy only to be displayed. The core reality of Christianity is found in establishing a complete relationship with Jesus Christ. This cannot be done with hit and miss encounters with Him, but only as a life-long process that takes time, trust, and commitment. The substance of life, what it really matters, is found in living and embracing all of it. This is crucial: it is where the work is done, the relationship is developed, and the volumes of a life are written upon your very heart and soul.

We cannot lengthen or shorten the time we have been allotted here on earth. However, we can live the life set before us by growing in the knowledge of the One who gives meaning to life. Take some time and sit down with the King of kings and see what you are made of and why you are here. You will be rewarded with a life that speaks not only of yourself, but also of the Lord and Savior Jesus Christ.

XXXII

FAITH

Behold the proud, His soul is not upright in him; but the just shall live by his faith.

Habakkuk 2:4

We have two phrases in our church that, although they pertain to men, speak generally to our faith as Christians. They are "man eyes" and "man ears", by which we mean the inability to see or hear something that is directly in front of you or spoken directly to you. (Sorry men, most of us will find our pictures under this entry if it were in the dictionary). The word faith has had volumes written about it; we use this word daily. Yet many suffer with man eyes and man ears in understanding exactly what it means. Faith determines how we see and what we hear. Let us take a very brief look at this word in order to hear it speak to us.

Faith is real and is absolutely necessary for a strong relationship with Jesus. Without faith, it is impossible to please God (Hebrews 11:6). Also, faith provides direction and reveals God, but without it there is no approaching Him, no forgiveness, no deliverance, no salvation, no communion, nor any spiritual life. Without faith, we are empty.

The Apostle Paul tells us that we walk by faith, not by sight (2 Corinthians 5:7). The problem is that we often struggle with our natural instincts and only see what we can see with our physical eyes and hear with our physical ears—causing us to shut out the spiritual. The result is that we run ahead of the cloud of God's providence and end up on a fool's errand, distracted and confused. We can also deny the reality of the One true God and insist on trusting, depending, and putting our faith in things of the world that will one day pass away (see 2 Corinthians 4:18).

Romans 1:17 tells us: "For in it the righteousness of God is revealed from faith to faith; as it is written, 'The just shall live by faith.'" This faith to faith reminds us that faith is not only the starting point of salvation, it is also the staying power in life. A person's faith in Jesus Christ grabs the heart—then the eyes and ears will follow. Faith is the way to a new life sourced only from Him and will guide a person in all and through all.

As a Christian, I do not live with man eyes and ears. I exist on the absolute assurance that God is the creator and ruler of all things, the provider and giver of eternal life through Christ. As I grasp that small measure of faith given to all believers (see Romans 12:3) my eyes are opened to Him to see what is important and critical.

Faith is the currency of eternity. God wants us to be rich people. Faith calls to us from what happened on the cross and provides us with the ability to see and hear our Savior. Faith also gives us insight and produces within us the ability to live in a world crippled by sin, while at the same time, casting our hearts upon heaven. Faith is love, it is real, and it is a life changer!

XXXIII

The Essentials

I have not departed from the commandment of His lips; I have treasured the words of His mouth more than my necessary food.

Job 23:12

I'm not much of a "butcher, baker, or candlestick maker." As a singer, a simple joyful noise to the Lord will suffice for me. As a musician with any sense of rhythm, clapping is my limit. Although not talented with these skills, I do know that these activities require essential components to be done well. Butchers use specific instruments, cooks follow detailed recipes, and musicians follow musical scales that are pleasing to the ear. Accomplishing these activities requires precision and patience to achieve the desired results. The same is true in Christianity: believers need to learn, through a relationship with Christ, how to establish a bedrock foundation of their faith. These essentials are often neglected.

Something that is essential can be defined as a basic element of highest importance that is needed to achieve a goal. An essential in Christ's Kingdom is growing as a follower and learning the teachings of Jesus Christ. Today, through this neglect, many personal foundations are shifty and many see no need to achieve something greater in their lives. If they do, their desires are quickly extinguished due to their weak foundation in the knowledge of the Word that is unable to support growth. The lack of discipleship results in many so-called

Christians who spiritually sleep away their life on earth. In doing so, they are wasting not only their own potential, but also the potential that lies within others that they should be connected to.

Some of the essential teaching topics of Christianity that we all need to know and be familiar with are: the Father, the Son, the Holy Spirit, divine judgment, suffering for the sake of Christ, prayer, forgiveness, obedience, love, the gifts of the Holy Spirit, and the spirit realm. Reading the Bible cover-to-cover is the only way to understand each of these items; although, because the Bible is living and active, an entire lifetime is not enough to ever completely understand it. Reading the Bible is required for growth and strength in our faith. Trust me when I say, this daily essential will soon become your most favorite part of the day as Holy Spirit comes to teach you through what you read.

There are no shortcuts to gain this knowledge. We gain understanding about God, not so much for the sake of acquiring information but for the sake of growing in His love. The greatest need we have is not to do things but to believe things. Then, in the believing will come the doing, the loving.

When you start to immerse your life in these essentials, you will see how they all fit together, how one leads to another, and that they all are sourced out from God. This understanding creates a life that doesn't choose to settle for average comfort but instead chooses to love. Unconditional love, the very heart of God Himself, is the foundation that truth rests upon and cannot be moved.

XXXIV

THE RIDDLE OF DEATH

O Death, where is your sting? O Hades, where is your victory?

1 Corinthians 15:55

Being a pastor, I have the opportunity to preside over wedding ceremonies and memorial services. Marrying is the subject of many jokes, yet there are few jokes told about dying. Why? When someone dies, we are reminded of our own mortality. The finality that comes at the end of our lives leaves us with a sense of complete helplessness. Death stings. Losing a loved one cuts us deeply, often leaving a permanent scar. Billy Graham speaks volumes toward understanding life and death: "We cannot begin to understand the riddle of death without the guiding knowledge of the Word of God. Outside of the Bible, death will forever remain an unknown phantom, stalking helpless human beings."[5]

The "riddle of death" can strike anybody, anytime, anywhere. Times of loss, regardless of how long the person lived, reminds us that life is short. Our society foolishly tries to find the fountain of youth but these vain attempts to push back death waste the precious time of many people. It keeps them outside of will of God and His Word.

Suffering loss is a part of life. Only a fool would think they could live above death or ignore it. The Word of God helps us to better understand death. Although, it doesn't always give us the specific answers we need about death, it does address the principles about it that can bring us great comfort.

Nothing will ever surprise God. When we are under His teaching, love, and protection we should not fear death. A person can experience incredible clarity when living through a time of loss. This realization of what really matters allows us to see what we cling to so tightly.

Without the guiding knowledge of the Word of God, a person will forever be helpless: stalked by death, stung by loss, and seeking comfort while trying to cover up the pain. A close relationship with Jesus Christ clarifies life, providing meaning and purpose, and relief during loss.

XXXV

The Brokenhearted

The LORD is near to the brokenhearted and saves those who are crushed in spirit.

Psalm 34:18 (NASB)

Be it a glass, a tooth, or the occasional bone, we all have done our share of breaking things. The reality of life is that brokenness can and will occur regardless of how careful we are. Unfortunately, when items get broken, sometimes they cannot be repaired.

What can break a heart? The most common causes are the loss of a loved one and losing something that holds tremendous personal value. This can leave us with a heart full of cracks and voids that initially appear to be beyond repair. Psalm 34:18 says that the LORD is close to those who are in desperate situations. We can find comfort in His arms.

Heart surgery is a specialized field that requires many years of schooling and experience. You would not have an eye doctor work on your heart or a veterinarian read your stress test. So why would you consult anything but the Bible and God's advice when your heart is damaged through suffering? Our society thinks they can analyze every situation and prescribe all kinds of medication to solve any problem, but this approach only puts a Band-Aid on a severe wound. God created you and He alone knows the intricacies of your heart. So, who better is there to heal your heart?

The Brokenhearted

The promise you have been given by God Himself is: "He heals the brokenhearted and binds up their wounds" (Psalm 147:3). Most broken bones and surgeries leave a body weaker than it originally was. When God comes on the scene, He takes a fragmented heart, puts it back together with such love, compassion, and care that it is much stronger than it was before. It can then endure more, do more, and love more.

The first step in the healing process is to trust God enough to give Him the damaged heart. If this is not done, a person will go through life forever fractured, living in a daily existence of anguish and tremendous pain. If your heart is crushed and needs repair, place it into the hands of God and allow Him to slowly bring it back to life with His love.

XXXVI

HAPPILY EVER AFTER

Oh, give thanks to the LORD! Call upon His name; make known His deeds among the peoples!

1 Chronicles 16:8

Aesop's Fables and other fairy tales provide a certain escape from reality. For children, it is the chance to believe that there are such places—realms where unicorns play, dragons roar, knights do battle, and Jack with his beanstalk and the golden goose live. These imaginings soon crumble when the age of innocence is trampled on by the cruel facts of a world corrupted by sin and ruled by those who crush dreams. Most people would like to live a life in the world of "Happily Ever After," seeking happiness which comes and goes without a reason or a warning.

I appreciate a good fairy tale, fantasy story, or the occasional sci-fi novel. Many skeptics consider the Bible to be in this same genre. They view the Bible to be nothing but mere fantasy that only a fool would believe, much less live by! The Bible has been relentlessly attacked through the ages, yet it has stood the test of time. It is based on history and is grounded in facts. It is the only book that can transplant unhappiness with joy.

There are certain things in this world that people like to overlook in their pursuit of happiness: God, satan, sin, judgment, heaven, and hell. As non-negotiable realities, simply disregarding them doesn't make them any less true. Satan certainly helps to disguise these realities through temporary promises of happiness in order to lure individuals into a permanent place of eternal torment.

Disneyland is a great place for a visit since it is "The Happiest Place on Earth." However, no one can stay there; at the end of the day everybody must leave and go home. The same is true for all of us here on earth. There is a time when we all must go. Then the reality of heaven and hell becomes either an anticipation or a horror. We choose how we live, and these choices will determine where we spend eternity. "Happily Ever After" only exists in heaven.

Jesus is the reality that all people need but few people find. He is real, He is love, and He wants you—now. This world is unable to provide "Happily Ever After," but Jesus can and will—forever! He will change your temporary happiness into eternal joy.

XXXVII

MISUNDERSTANDINGS

God did not send His Son into the world to condemn the world, but that the world through Him might be saved.

John 3:17

There are many things in this world that I understand, and then, there are others things that I never will. Some questions I have are: Why do people like to shop? How can sweets and cookies be so small yet hold so many calories? Perhaps one of the most misunderstood events in the history of the world is the birth of Jesus Christ. He never claimed to be anything other than the Son of God, who came into this world to die for all, cleansing us from our sin and by His grace giving us the gift of eternal life to all who believe in Him.

Make no mistake, Jesus lived His life as an example for us to follow. He came down and left a legacy for us to inherit through a relationship with Him. People make a classic mistake when they deny their sinful heritage, pursuing instead a life built on a foundation of standards that shift and sway with the time.

The revelation of Jesus seems to be playing in the background of many people's minds, yet His worth has become marginalized, comercialized, or wiped out. As society hungrily shops for satisfaction that money can't buy, Jesus cries out to them not from the empty manger, but from what He did on the cross. It on the cross where His love was poured out to give the clear and simple gift of eternal life.

Misunderstandings

My Father in heaven sent a newborn Child into this world over 2,000 years ago. This act was not a mistake but rather a statement of love. To those who believe in Him, Jesus is not only the best but also the biggest gift of all time. Let there be no misunderstanding, His message of eternal life still rings clear and is freely offered to all.

XXXVIII

GOD IS LOVE

He who does not love does not know God, for God is love.

1 John 4:8

Love can be fickle, disappointing, and fade away just like the changing seasons. The love that the world praises is ultimately meaningless and directionless. It leaves a person panicked, empty, cold, bitter, and fat. On the other hand, God is love. He alone has what we are longing for. His love is precious and permanent. It will not disappoint, and it provides the ability for us to see Him and others with compassion. His love is healthy. It will truly heal the broken heart. God is love.

The heart is a muscle that we must protect through exercise so that it stays healthy and strong. It also needs to be protected as the emotional epicenter of the soul. In this capacity, a heart that is energetic will be engaged with others but will also be wounded in the process of living and loving. This is not only the work of the world but also the desire of the Father. Our hearts become stronger when they are mended by the loving hands of God. Through this process, we learn how to love better with a depth, width, and height that exhibits the distinct qualities of God's love.

It is easy for an inactive heart to become complacent, self-centered and hard. People with idle hearts may have been wounded in the past and do not want to present themselves to the torment of the world.

They hide their hearts and tuck them away in the dark until they are barely beating. C.S. Lewis says this about a heart in this condition:

> There is no safe investment. To love at all is to be vulnerable. Love anything, and your heart will certainly be wrung and possibly be broken. If you want to make sure of keeping it intact, you must give your heart to no one, not even to an animal. Wrap it carefully round with hobbies and little luxuries; avoid all entanglements; lock it up safe in the casket or coffin of your selfishness. But in that casket—safe, dark, motionless, airless—it will change. It will not be broken; it will become unbreakable, impenetrable, irredeemable. The alternative to tragedy, or at least to the risk of tragedy, is damnation. The only place outside heaven where you can be perfectly safe from all the dangers and perturbations (worries) of love is Hell.[6]

Our hearts desire fellowship with others—to be held and to hold the love of another. The true heart of Godly love grows stronger as it learns to love through encounters with pain, suffering and death. This is the heart God wants to establish in His people; it is the heart that freely presented itself on the cross and was pierced by a Roman spear for all mankind. That was the heart of God, the sinless Man who loved like nobody else, for everybody else. If you truly desire love, get to know the Author of it.

XXXIX

CRISIS

"I will look to the LORD; I will wait for the God of my salvation; My God will hear me."

Micah 7:7

Crisis is a word that brings many different images to the mind. For some, it can be as simple as a bad hair day or failing an exam, but for others it is a debilitating disease or death. Whatever form it takes, a crisis appears quickly, often without notice, and needs to be dealt with immediately. God originally made this world perfect, but then it all started to go downhill with Adam's decision to disobey God. We are now born into a world that is constantly in crisis: filled with emergencies, disasters, and violence. Thankfully, God remedied this problem by sending His Only Son to intervene and save all those who come to Him from eternal death. This is crisis intervention at the Biblical level.

The once good world created by the very hands of God now bear the scars inflicted upon it by the hands of humanity. Our perspective of the creation account directly determines if we will become a victim of the crisis or if we will persevere and endure. We can also amplify a crisis by fanning the flames to make it worse. This often becomes the situation when we immediately react in our own power and rely on God as a last resort or not at all.

A crisis, no matter its form, brings a potent and sometimes lethal punch that can only be softened and removed by the loving hand of God. Hebrews tells us that "faith is the substance of things hoped for, the evidence of things not seen" (Hebrews 11:1). This is an awesome verse to live by, but when we are under the thumb of a serious illness we tend to look and see only the situation, losing ourselves in it. This leaves us with a very different view—despair, the evidence of things seen, the substance of hopelessness—that is contrary to what God wants us to see.

Many misunderstand why Jesus came into the world. He didn't come to make evil people good. Jesus came to make dead people alive! His life, ministry, and crucifixion cleared the way for those who cannot see through their pain and despair. There is no other source of hope—past, present, or future—apart from Jesus Christ. The facts are clearly laid out in all of history: He came for us, He loves us, He desires all to come to Him, and He is the very King of the crisis, now and forever!

XL

THE THINKING BOX

Your faith should not be in the wisdom of men but in the power of God.

1 Corinthians 2:5

"Thinking outside the box" became a popular phrase in the late 1970s and is still common today. It means to have a vision beyond the basics, the status quo, and to forge ahead to come up with something new. While trying to think "outside the box," there is one thing that many people overlook: it cannot be done effectively until there is a very good idea what is "inside the box."

As a Christian and as a simple man who lives in a complex and constantly changing world, I am able to find the basics of everything I need in the Bible. God's Word is the box from which we all should operate and draw our strength from. However, it is not the Bible alone that gives us strength, but putting the truths discovered inside the box to use while operating outside the box.

A Biblical knowledge of God will compel you to step out of your box in order to work for Him. This means going, reaching, helping, holding, and showing love to all. The reality of the road to eternal life is that it is narrow, rough, and filled with danger and adventure. When you move outside in faith, not seeking to preserve your own self-interests, you suddenly become aware of how large the road becomes. The seemingly black and white everyday world is now filled with color, purpose, and love.

The Thinking Box

I like the concept of thinking outside the box. I was on the outside for many years without the proper tools; tinkering in life while enjoying success yet always looking for that One thing that was missing. Life was always good for me, but with God it is now great! With my new inside the box understanding (which has changed the inside of me), I am able to provide outside the box support to others. Take the time to know Him before venturing out on your own. You will never be disappointed and will forever be changed.

XLI

THE LAND IN BETWEEN

While we do not look at the things which are seen, but at the things which are not seen. For the things which are seen are temporary, but the things which are not seen are eternal.

2 Corinthians 4:18

We often find ourselves between things as we breathe, move, and exist on this earth. This in-between place could be somewhere as simple as between meals, between destinations, or between classes. We can also find ourselves in more difficult places, such as between jobs, between relationships, or "caught between a rock and a hard place." Every person who has ever lived on this planet finds themselves between two places of eternity—either on the road to the Promised Land (heaven) or on, as AC/DC sang, "A Highway to Hell."

The Land in Between is the territory we occupy on the way to our eternal destination. In this land, we find some places laid up with milk and honey and others filled with rotten fruit and horrific odors. Some Christians fool themselves by fabricating their own permanent place on earth through careers, possession, and obsessions. The reality is that these things always change. The loss that comes through this alteration can produce a bitter experience and defeated attitude in the life of the believer. If the true disciple of the crucified Christ loses sight of the totality of the gospel and their Lord and Savior, the Land in Between can be the place where faith goes to die.

This world is constantly changing. The pursuit of happiness alone will continually disappoint and eventually become exhausting. The solutions to all our problems can be said to lie just around the corner. Unfortunately, for many that corner never comes. Life becomes second-rate and the Land in Between becomes a desert where a person's desires and thirsts can never be fully satisfied.

The Land in Between is a land that produces pleasures, money, relationships, and other temporary items. It is also a place filled with hunger, disease, and where the most permanent appointment we all must face can be found: death. A person cannot acknowledge the reality of heaven without acknowledging the dreadful certainty of hell. These are both eternal destinations. Each individual will decide where they will reside while living life here on earth. Have you?

XLII

THANKS

Oh, give thanks to the LORD, for He is good!

Psalm 106:1

A good definition of "thankful" is one that contains such words as grateful and kindness in both giving and receiving. The true substance of the word is found in acknowledging something that is received. Whether it's a big-ticket item or small purchase, the effect of receiving a gift is impressed upon our lives by the act itself. By embracing the deed—neither neglecting the action nor taking it for granted, but rather purposefully placing it in our heart where it cannot be forgotten—we are blessed by the gift. The true worth of receiving a gift is realized when the action sinks in to make an imprint upon the soul.

Thankfulness grows in the heart. As our heart becomes larger, we lose the expectation that things will be given to us and more fully receive them as what they truly are—gifts of greatness and treasures of kings, which are precious to behold. From this place of maturity, the act of receiving produces gratefulness in our heart leading us to become the giver of things, all because we became thankful receivers. Gratefulness permanently marks our heart by placing value on the person as well the item received from them.

Thanks

It is said that "Giving is better than receiving" and I won't argue with that; nevertheless, this process starts with us truly understanding and cultivating thankfulness. This attitude is a very affordable item that pays dividends beyond measure. Jesus freely gave for us all, so that we would be able to receive eternal life. Please take it, let it grow, and pass it on to others. You will still have plenty for yourself!

XLIII

HE IS WHO HE IS

Suddenly a voice came from heaven, saying, "This is My beloved Son, in whom I am well pleased."

Matthew 3:17

There are many popular phrases that have come and gone with time. Being the "cat's pajamas" in the 1920s was better than hearing someone say, "I'll be a monkey's uncle!" the following decade. The 40s came in with "cool" and "smooch." If you were a "hipster" in the 50s then it probably wasn't easy to "keep up with the Joneses" in the 60's You might "dig it" or be caught on "the flip side" in the 70's. Whoever came up with "gag me with a spoon" in the 80's hopefully also said "my bad" in the 90's. The turn of the century heard "peeps" and "newbies" while today you might say "it is what it is"—a phrase that doesn't really mean anything. Slang is the ultimate escape of communicating with others. People throw it around to sometimes explain the unexplainable but other times to flee responsibility and personal accountability.

Jesus Christ addressed the doubters of His day by taking them to task regarding who He was. There was no room for doubt about His identity when He quoted the Scripture "I Am who I Am" (Exodus 3:14). The translation of this phrase in Hebrew is, *Yehovah*, which means "the Eternal Living God." Jesus left no room for misunderstanding or ducking the truth. Everyone is accountable to Him alone. Directly confronted by the sin in their lives, the religious leaders refused to deal with the truth that Jesus offered. The truth demanded a change of allegiance to Him alone.

On judgment day a "cool" phrase will not "fly" when you stand face to face with Jesus Christ. He won't settle for an "it is what it is" excuse for your neglected relationship with Him. The world of baseball gets it right, "you are either in or out." You cannot live your life "on the fence"—you are either destined for heaven or hell.

Out of great love for us, Jesus left the world with no excuse for not knowing Him. His clear message of redemption avoids any confusion we might have. Some people attempt to ignore the Eternal Living God in order to avoid a confrontation with their own wicked hearts. Despite misperceptions, a pile of religions, and different paths to heaven, the reality remains that all of these roads lead to the gates of hell.

Jesus loves us so much that He came to earth to show us who God is and that He is who He claims to be—the giver of eternal life. He is who He is, the great "I am"—which is the greatest phrase of all time!

XLIV

Paper Hearts

Keep yourselves in the love of God, looking for the mercy of our Lord Jesus Christ unto eternal life.

Jude 1:21

I recently had the opportunity to do a last-minute substitute teaching job in elementary art. The morning consisted of helping several kindergarten classes cut out paper hearts and place them on a large piece of paper. These large valentines were then to be signed with a simple "I Love You." I'm not one to over spiritualize everything in my life or to look for sermon topics to force feed to the next unsuspecting individual. However, I couldn't get over the concern, care, and joy these young kids had in making these paper hearts for the people they loved. This simple activity conveyed so much meaning.

Simple things, the things that don't contain worldly interference and clutter, seem to always carry the most weight. Through the care these kids took in making paper hearts, they demonstrated the depth of love they had for others. They were so happy making a valentine for the one they loved, yet panicked in their inability to create the most perfectly-shaped heart. The attention these kids had for such a simple thing opened my eyes and touched my soul.

Although the technically-perfect heart was the one without any ragged edges; to the recipient, its real worth would be determined by the hand that held the scissors. These kids displayed various states of fear and frustration when they cut out something that didn't represent a heart at all. When I revealed to some of them with a few extra clips that there was indeed a heart in that piece of paper, they showed great joy! We shared a sacred moment without even realizing what was taking place.

It was not a precise lesson plan nor a scripted exercise. Instead it was a very personal and purposeful time. Glue sticks, scissors, pencils, and a few extra kid-made hearts that were tucked away in my shirt pocket carried the day for me. This experience can remind us all that life is far from perfect. Our hearts are clipped, nipped, and formed lovingly by the hand of God. We sometimes panic and become fearful that our lives are not shaping up the way we plan them to, but when we realize that God is handling the scissors, the internal pressure eases as He slowly shapes our hearts. Christianity is simply believing that Jesus Christ died on a cross, was buried, and rose to life again as the Son of God. It is a simple thing, just like paper hearts.

XLV

WHY? TO WHAT?

He said to them, "But who do you say that I am?"

Matthew 16:15

A simple one-word question starts out innocently enough very early in life; although, it quickly becomes ingrained in the very nature of our beings. We ask this one particular question sometimes with suspicion and other times quite honestly, but either way, it forever remains on the edge of our consciousness. The question is "Why?"

Unfortunately, "Why?" can be the glue that keeps our eyes fixed on us. "Why?" has the power to blind and bind us to a problem until it seems that there is no way out. "Why?" can be selfish, miss the point, and blame God. Asking "Why?" has the ability to isolate anyone and can be filled with suspicion and mistrust.

God wants to transform our questioning of Him from a position of suspicion to a position of expectation. This repositioning changes many of our "Why?" questions into "What?" questions. The movement from "Why?" to "What?" occurs through trusting and obeying God. It involves God's love growing and moving in the core of our lives. This progression is not instantaneous; it is a process we experience over time. Instead of relying on our own natural abilities, we turn to God. "Why are you are doing this to me?" changes to "What is this for, Lord?" and "What do you want me to see, learn, and do, Lord?"

By entering the realm of asking "What?", we are able to cast our cares upon God, who is our Sustainer. Instead of accusing Him we are asking for His guidance, wisdom, and help because He is the best resource in existence. "What?" shows trust and willingness to grow in relationship with God. It requires constant communication that keeps us moving forward with eyes open and hands out. "What?" will demand action on our part, since the answer may not be entirely dependent on God. It is our participation in understanding how He works in our lives that fills the emptiness in us and overflows to others.

XLVI

Dear Father

He said to them, "When you pray, say: Our Father in heaven, hallowed be Your name. Your kingdom come. Your will be done on earth as it is in heaven."

Luke 11:2

Dear Heavenly Father,

First and foremost, I want to always be thankful for everything You have done and ever will do for me. I am sorry for unfairly stealing divine glory for what You have accomplished in my life and for the times I did not take responsibility of my own actions. I greatly appreciate those occasions when You answered my prayer with a "No." In hindsight it is easy to see that my requests were not in Your best interest and would have either hurt or destroyed me.

Father, I treasure the days You have gifted to me, including those of drudgery when I was able to better absorb who You are and learn how to survive on Your absolute goodness and power. I am starting to understand that trials test my character in order to reveal who You are and Your light to the dying world through me.

I am so grateful for how you continue to show me who You are and that You have patience with me during this process of life. You are always near when I need You, even in the times when I think that you are not. Lord, strengthen me to do Your will and help me to not demand my own way. May the world see the reality of You in me. Help me not to pretend to be someone that I am not nor to make You out to be someone You are not. Let me not treat You merely as a way to gain the items that I want while clinging tightly to things that aren't needed.

I cannot describe the new heart You have given to me upon my believing in Your Son Jesus Christ as Lord. It has absorbed life's crippling losses, separation, and hurt, as well as constantly teaching me how to forgive and to love. I know these are just the mere edges of Your ways and yet You leave me desiring more time to look, pray, and walk with You.

Heavenly Father, these are but a few words that attempt to describe how much You mean to me. Please develop in my heart a love for the lost, a prayer for those who hate, and above all, a desire to never give in to sin by following You all the days of my life. I look forward to coming home to heaven and finally being able to meet You face to face. Until then, I will fight the good fight, for to live is Christ and to die is nothing but gain.

XLVII

Note To Self

Jesus said to them, "My food is to do the will of Him who sent Me, and to finish His work."

John 4:34

I love to write things down. It is my attempt to learn and remember as much as humanly possible. Lists, Bible verses, numbers, etc.—many of these find their way into the note section of my phone; others are written on scraps of paper, put in my pocket, forgotten, and later destroyed by the washing machine. If I would pen a note to myself with regards to cementing my relationship with Jesus, it would be, "Set the purpose of Jesus before me and everything else will fall into place." That is my intent, to be obedient to the will of God by doing it. Anything else is quiet rebellion.

A note to self: I do not want to string together days without meaning, as this leads to a life without substance and obstructs all avenues of understanding. I will look to God's greater purpose and avoid diluting my effectiveness with meaningless activity. Living any other way will trap me in the desert, the valley of death, where there is no god to deliver me. Living in this way is wasteful and empty. It produces a stone-cold heart and a bitter love.

A note to self: Beware of being tricked into cheap substitutes. These use traps that appear to deliver, but then only yield a certain slow death to the soul. Human religions are hollow systems that glorify man and degrade God. They promise false deliverance from an irreconcilable war through a program that is only a cover for ignorance. The actual result yields only unanswered questions as the real resolution lies beyond the reach of individual ability.

A note to self: I must die daily in order to obey God and discover what He has for me eternally. My ability to stay moldable is accomplished exclusively during the time I spend with God and in His word. Look for the good in people, as the bad is proudly displayed and hate is the new love language embraced by the world.

A note to all: Having every reason to live for God, don't choose to do so without Him. It takes a list of commitments and an effort to follow through with this. Obedience is the polar opposite of quiet rebellion. Do what you can, when you can, with all you have. Even in your exhaustion, exalt God. You can do extraordinary things if you spend time with Jesus. True theology brings understanding; experiencing His love brings power.

P.S. Living is all about Jesus.

XLVIII

My Own Little Place

Whenever I am afraid, I will trust in You.

Psalm 56:3

There is a place I have enjoyed going to. It is fabricated in the imagination of my soul. This place has no boundaries and holds everything that I require. Time there is not rushed, and I receive all my desires upon asking. I stand on a floating surface of some sort, and I know that there is a sky, although it is never seen. "Never" or "maybe" do not exist here and everything is available to me for my own personal benefit. It is a very fine place. This was not only a very necessary place for me, but a space of learning as well.

Yet, I have noticed a problem within this place. For all its apparent perfection, it immediately falls to pieces and ceases to exist when my imagination collides with reality. Selfish imagination and reality are mutually exclusive and cannot coexist. My imaginary place has tremendous appeal; however, I notice that its largeness shrinks quickly as I return to the land of the living. Conflicts that do not belong here find their way in. Boundaries that I wish away return, and I begin to see a very real foundation and a sky. "No" does exist, everything I desire quickly disappears, time ticks by and all things are no longer just for me.

There is a new place that I live in now: a spirit-filled reality that is constantly learning to align with the will of God. It is filled with both my ideas and my insights. It is both heaven and earth— having the ability to coexist in both heaven and earth is given to me by the Creator God of the universe. Entering this new place was made possible by Jesus upon my repenting of sins and exchanging my desires for His. This new place exposes and destroys unnecessary individual thoughts that make demands upon the soul that cannot be fulfilled outside of its Creator. It is a place of individual choice where mistakes can be made and are forgiven.

There are countless destinations we all go to during our lives, yet deep down in everyone's soul there is a longing to occupy this new place. We want to be home with our Creator. Don't let your imagination create a reality that does not exist. Instead, let your little private place become His big eternal home.

XLIX

The Man Who Taught Me How to Forgive

Jesus said to him, "I do not say to you, up to seven times, but up to seventy times seven."

Matthew 18:22

One of the most difficult concepts the world deals with is forgiveness. The concept of forgiveness creates turmoil and difficulty in the natural man as well as in the person who has given their life to Jesus Christ. Each one of us have daily opportunities to forgive. They come in many forms. Forgiveness demands action from those of us who seek it out, but requires nothing from the one who caused the hurt.

The notion of forgiveness is hard to deal with since it is often misunderstood. Forgiveness must be seen through the eyes of God and is defined by Him alone. In forgiving someone, you are not condoning sin; you are simply letting God deal with it. That is His turf, not yours. It is easier to offer forgiveness to others when you realize how much you've been forgiven. By forgiving, you are not saying that what was done is right, rather you are saying that you are not going to let what was done rule over your life any longer. You are giving it to God—where it rightly belongs. He will take it and heal you.

Forgiveness is an action that can only be effectively engaged under the blood of Christ. You must hand your hurt and wounding to Him.

Your old nature must be put to death and buried. If it's not, then that old nature will take you to the gates of hell and back again in an endless loop. Although forgiveness is not easy, it is necessary. If you are dealing with the issue of forgiveness, give it to Jesus and let Him nail your confessions to the cross. He commanded it, demanded it, and lived it. That is what Jesus' life is all about.

L

FENCES

Before faith came, we were kept under guard by the law, kept for the faith which would afterward be revealed. Therefore the law was our tutor to bring us to Christ, that we might be justified by faith. But after faith has come, we are no longer under a tutor.

Galatians 3:23-25

No matter where you live or what you do, you cannot escape the restriction or protection of fences. These barriers seem to be everywhere and anywhere. Some are placed with obvious reason while others reveal no apparent thought. One thing is for certain, their existence is for a purpose, and before they are moved or destroyed, the question of why they are present needs to be answered. Fences of morality, otherwise known as rules, are often broken due to their restrictive nature. Rule breakers don't realize that these guardrails restrain evil that is determined to destroy them by flooding in and out of their lives.

I live in cattle ranching territory, a land of thousands of miles of fencing. A standard rule in this part of the country is that if you open a gate, you always close it behind you. These fences exist for a reason: they are put in place to keep some cattle in and to keep other cattle out. They are there as barriers of protection for both what is inside and what is outside. The same can be said of the laws and guidelines given to us by God in the Bible. What the modern world thinks of as old and holding little value actually provides all of creation with the ultimate protection from an enemy of wickedness that never ages.

God is love. He does not place restrictions on us and give us rules to live by because He is closed-minded and hateful. He puts all things in place because He loves us and wants to protect us from harmful activities of others and ourselves. Fences, rules, and boundaries are not only needed for a society to function properly; they are critical!

I like a nice protective fence and appreciate a shut door when I sleep at night. Most people lock their car doors, place their money in a bank, and rely heavily on passwords. The protective boundaries of God are meant to comfort us in the same way. God has lovingly written His law on our hearts, both individually and collectively. When these fences are ignored, removed, or replaced there is absolutely nothing defending society from evil. Love is the reason these fences were put in place by the Creator of all.

¹ God in the Dock. C.S. Lewis. William B. Eardmans Publishing Co. UK. 1970, p. 52.

² Humility. The Journey Toward Holiness. Andrew Murray. Bethany House Publishers. 11400 Hampshire Ave. South, Bloomington, MN 55438. 2006. p.16.

³ Leadership. J.R. Miller. Ed. Navpress Publishing Corp., 1987. ISBN: 9780891091899.

⁴ Mere Christianity. C.S. Lewis. Harper Collins, N.Y. 2001 p. 82.

⁵ Death and the Life After. Billy Graham. Thomas Neslon, Inc. Nashville, TN. 1987 p. 7.

⁶ The Four Loves, C.S. Lewis, New York: Harcourt, Brace, Jovanovich, 1960, pp. 169-170

Enjoy these books that are also from Red Door Sentinel, LLC.

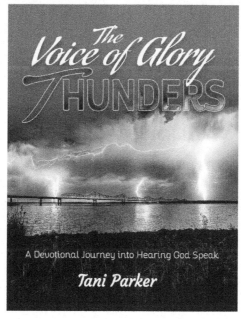

Made in the USA
Monee, IL
18 May 2021